Endeavor

Cultivate Excellence While Making a Difference

Scott Perry

ISBN-13: 978-1-7944-3739-5

Copy Editor: Lisa Perry

For my altMBA, The Marketing Seminar, and The Bootstrapper's Workshop friends and fellow travelers. I do what I do because you inform and inspire me with your generous work and example. Thank you.

Seth, Maya, Jenn, Marie, Brigitte, Fredrick, Louise, Francoise, Travis, Susan, and Jodi this work came to be because of your support and encouragement.
Thank you.

For Lisa, Spencer, and Emerson. You are the endeavor that matters most.

Table of Contents

A companion workbook and resource guide, *The Endeavor Project*, is available. To download the workbook, visit:

https://creativeonpurpose.mykajabi.com/theendeavorproject
info

Preface - It's Time to Make a Difference

You are enough.

Yet, capable of more.

We need you.

It's time to make a difference.

It's time to fly higher.

Choices

Haven't you wasted enough time traveling the well-worn path of what's expected?

Are you done seeking a destination mapped out by the status quo and leading to where everyone else is headed?

Do you want to settle for the tried and true, the ordinary, and the unremarkable?

Or are you ready to chart a course and draw a map of your own?

Draw Your Own Map

It's time to embark on a voyage of discovery. Who are you? What are you good at? Where do you belong?

You've answered these questions before. But, you're not the same person, nor in the same situation, and not surrounded by the same people now as you were then.

Answers to these questions aren't found on the map everyone else is following. They're discoveries made with a compass.

This book is a compass to help you draw your own map. *Endeavor* shares a process that encourages you to step into your "what's next" with integrity and intention.

This isn't a self-help book. It's a help-others book.

You enhance your life most when you engage in work that serves others. You find that work at the intersection of your values, talents, and tribe.

It's time to fly higher in an endeavor that makes a difference.

Are you ready?

What Is an Endeavor?

It's more than a hobby, but not necessarily your job or role. It's a vocation found at the intersection of who you are, what you're good at, and where you belong. An endeavor is work that you are *meant* to do *now*.

An endeavor cultivates gratitude because you don't have to do it, you *get* to do it. It also generates appreciation in others because it is a gift generously shared with those who need it.

Endeavors shun the status quo. These efforts intend to transform. Endeavors strive to help people get from where they are to where they want to be.

Endeavors cultivate fulfillment and well-being. They align who you are, what you do, and where you belong. These enterprises encourage a sense of passion and purpose. Endeavors inform a healthy perspective about your status and level of prosperity.

You might luck out and "wander" into a vocation, but a thoughtful approach gives you better odds of developing and delivering work that is significant and satisfying.

Here's a Venn diagram of how you can identify *your* next endeavor.

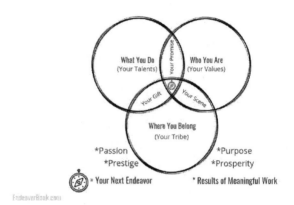

This book shares an approach to identify, develop, and deliver work that makes a difference. It's not a checklist, nor a step-by-step system. It's a set of concepts and practices developed through my journey as a husband, father, teacher, and musician that helps me thrive every day.

The approach laid out here is also honed through my coaching practice and the work I do as a coach in online programs created by Seth Godin. *Everything* shared here has helped countless others experience a greater sense of well-being and fulfillment while navigating a challenging journey into what's next.

Let's unpack this process. But first, a question.

Actually, a few questions.

Before You Begin - Why Are You Here?

This book shares concepts and a process for finding meaning through work that makes a difference. The kind of enterprise done with and for others. The assertion made here is that you enhance your life through work that serves others.

Again, *Endeavor* isn't a self-help book. It's a help-others book.

It's impossible to identify meaningful work without first giving some thought to the meaning of life.

Before diving into how to find your "what's next," consider the three questions on the following pages.

Write your answers in this book if you like. Or jot them down in the companion workbook. Or respond in a journal, digital or leather bound. Or record yourself talking them over with friends and family. It's less important *how* you do answer these questions than it is *that* you answer them.

Human beings have asked these questions for millennia and continue to seek answers. There are no absolutely "right" answers to these queries, just "alright" responses for right now.

Don't get hung up on this exercise and don't return this book for a refund. At least not yet. Give these questions a try. Your next endeavor depends on it.

What does it mean to be human?

What does it mean to be happy?

How can I be more of both?

At this point, you may well be asking yourself another question.

"What the Hell Have I Gotten Myself Into?"

Right now, you may feel doubtful, anxious, irritated, or just plain confused. "What does it mean to be human? I don't have time to think about this!" "What does it mean to be happy? I don't know what it *means* to be happy. I just want to *be* happy!"

If you want to return this book now, I don't blame you. Go ahead.

But, my intent isn't to fuel your anger or your angst. I want to inspire your curiosity. I seek to encourage you to engage your courage. I'm hoping these questions got a little under your skin. I'm hoping they made you lean in a bit more and wonder, "Where is all this heading?"

If you're ready to find out where this is going next, thinking about life's big questions can help you start dialing in answers to the inquiries coming up in Book I: "Who are you?" "What are you good at?" And, "Where do you belong?"

Before you begin answering those questions though, I'll put myself on the hook and share my answers.

Why I Think You're Here

That's right. I'm going to answer the same questions I asked you. Not because I have *the* answers. I definitely don't. But I do have *some* answers, and I assert that, although not definitive, they are good enough to get you started.

At the very least, I hope my answers inspire you to develop and share *your* answers to the three questions: "What does it mean to be human? What does it mean to be happy? And how can I be more of both?"

There are three things about what it means to be human with which I think you'll agree. You are an inherently social creature. You are born with the capacity for reason. And, you possess a creative impulse.

And by employing these instincts through meaningful endeavors, you can become more human and happy. You most enhance your life by elevating the lives of others.

You Are an Inherently Social Creature

Sure, there are plenty of examples of people leading solitary and self-sustaining lives. But at some point, they employ a tool, or idea, or resource that is not their own. We are born to live with and serve, others.

Our social instinct comes from an evolutionary imperative. When human beings first appeared on the scene, they were neither the fastest nor the strongest animal in the food chain. Alone, you'd likely end up as some other animal's lunch. But in a group, you could flip the tables on those that preyed upon you.

Fear and danger drove humans to become social creatures. And being social creatures made us develop our capacity for reason.

You Are Born With the Capacity for Reason

Yes, I know. It's easy to second guess our capacity for reason by pointing out the innumerable examples of our failure to employ it. Obviously, human beings possess impulses other than rational thinking that lead to irrational and unreasonable behavior. The capacity for reason is one thing, fostering it is quite another.

But there's no denying that our social nature informed our intellect and consciousness. Collaboration and cooperation require communication, and communication requires developing brain power.

Becoming social creatures gave us a chance for survival in a hostile world; furthering our capacity for reason provided the opportunity to dominate it.

And the combination of your social instinct and capacity for reason inform and inspire your creative impulse.

You Possess a Creative Impulse

Creativity is merely the act of bringing something forth that did not previously exist. Every time you make a meal, make a mess or make amends you employ your creative inclination.

Every significant undertaking you've ever engaged in employs your creative powers. Learning to walk, speak, write, or perform any other task draws on your creative abilities.

And your creative capacity is developed by learning as you go and amplified through doing work with others. That brings us right back to our social disposition and closes the virtuous cycle of what is required to be human and happy.

Creativity also informs the path to becoming more of both.

Back to the Question of "Why Are You Here?"

You may have picked this book up because it looked like a book about personal development. What is now called "life design." Or you might think it's about career design. Regardless, you likely found it in the Self-Help section of the bookstore, virtual or otherwise.

But this isn't a self-help book. It's a help-others book.

Because the only way you can truly improve your life is by enhancing the lives of others. You and those transformed by your endeavor are brothers and sisters, not by blood, but because of your social imperative, shared capacity for consciousness, and creative impulse.

Yes, that's an assertion. It can, and should be, investigated, questioned, and argued. But until you can make an overwhelming and compelling argument to the contrary, I encourage you to stick with this idea.

Your life can only be enhanced by engaging in work that serves others.

And the only way you can do that is to have some idea about who you are, what you're good at, and where you belong.

Book I - Agency & Assets

You are the hero in this endeavor. A journey that involves discovering who you are, what you're good at, and where you belong. It begins by taking stock of where you are now and then determining where you want to go next.

Chapter 1 - Who's In Charge?

"Happiness and freedom begin with a clear understanding of one principle. Some things are within our control, and some things are not." - Epictetus

Agency is as intoxicating as it is elusive. When the breaks go your way, it's easy to believe it's due to your intelligence and planning. When things go awry, it's easy to blame others or fate.

The truth is, very little is within your control, but at the same time, you *do* control *everything* required to maintain your sense of well-being and prosperity.

You ultimately control only two things. You determine *how* you choose to perceive yourself, others, and your situation. You also control what you decide to do next.

Everything else is beyond your control.

Your body is subject to disease, decline, and ultimately death. The attitude and behavior of others are for them to decide, not you. And there are forces far more powerful than you at work in the social, political, economic, cultural, and geographical arenas.

However, many things beyond your absolute control *are* within your *influence.*

You can eat well and exercise to promote a healthy body. You can adopt a compassionate posture toward others that encourage them to engage their goodness as well.

And you can choose your "battles" and leverage your assets to persuade results that enhance the prospects for all.

Speaking of assets, you'll take some personal asset inventories in the next chapter. Before then, let's look at an important one that you "own," but rarely prize as much as you should.

The Present Moment

You cannot change the past. At best, you can only hope to influence the future. Even then, you can't be sure if what you create will be genuinely beneficial.

The *only* time you possess agency is in the here and now. The present moment.

There is an opportunity for you *right now* to move into "what's next" with integrity and intention. Virtue and purpose are powerful levers. Employ them to amplify your message and broadcast your vision. These levers will increase the odds that the change you bring forth aligns with your values and vision.

The clearer you are about your motivations and aspirations, the more effectively and efficiently you can bring about the change you seek to make. When you mindfully dial in your values, talents, and tribe, you begin to enhance your own life through the work you do to improve the lives of others.

Before you identify your values, talents, and tribes, there are four essential practices you should cultivate in the here and now. Embracing and developing these habits ensures that you thrive *through* the challenges that lie ahead in developing and delivering your endeavor.

Gratitude, Generosity, & Grace

You probably pay lip service to these three words. You recognize that they're essential virtues. You'd like to see more of all three in the world. You want to nurture more of each within yourself.

The sooner you do the latter, the sooner you'll help initiate the former.

Even more critical, practicing gratitude, generosity, and grace cultivate the most important benefit and feature of an endeavor, compassion.

I've alluded to the idea that initiating an endeavor is beginning a hero's journey. Embracing gratitude, generosity, grace, and compassion adds a spiritual element to this "adventure." You'll feed the soul in addition to promoting physical health and psychological happiness.

Let's take a brief look at each of these assets and why you want to foster them.

Gratitude

Gratitude is the appreciation for what you have and receive. You may be grateful for a tangible object or an intangible concept. Regardless, when you mindfully and genuinely practice gratitude, there is science that points to profound benefits, not the least of which is a feeling of happiness.

Expressing gratitude acknowledges the goodness in your life. Even more, it helps you recognize that the source of that goodness lies outside of yourself. Gratitude cultivates a feeling of connection with others and something bigger than you.

Gratitude encourages you to contextualize yourself, your circumstances, and your surroundings within a broader framework that acknowledges others. Appreciation inspires a feeling of belonging and supports an unselfish perspective. This all leads to a more sustainable approach to what is "enough."

Gratitude boosts contentment, optimism, and resilience.

Be grateful.

Generosity

Generosity is the expression of kindness, understanding, and selflessness. It's an inherent impulse born of our social nature. This primal quality explains why giving and helping makes you feel good and why being selfish and stingy feels terrible. As with gratitude, there is good science supporting the assertion that generosity also boosts your health and happiness.

Generosity requires the recognition of others and therefore cultivates empathy and compassion. It leads to a feeling of "oneness" with others which enhances the experience and emotional health of both the giver and receiver.

Developing your generous nature enables you to move beyond need and desire. Generosity helps you recognize that you are, and already have, "enough." You already possess an *abundance* of gifts. These gifts only have meaning through developing and sharing them.

Generosity creates bonds, encourages collaboration, and fuels reciprocity.

Be generous.

Grace

Grace is the act of extending forgiveness or mercy. The word itself comes from the same root as that of gratitude and is embedded deeply into the practice of generosity. Grace requires and promotes excellence of character which includes both moral virtue and ethical will.

Grace is central to many of the world's religions and most impactful social movements. Turning the other cheek, forgiving those who harm you, and embracing anguish and misfortune are powerful and moving responses to trying situations.

Nothing is more challenging than the pursuit and practice of grace. That's why it's so valued and worth your persistent effort.

Only grace leads to enlightenment, wisdom, and transcendence. And grace begins with *you*.

How can you possibly extend forgiveness and mercy to others if you can't yet extend them to yourself? You are an imperfect being. A broken vessel carrying around a fragile soul. Be kind to yourself, and it will be much easier to extend kindness to others.

Be full of grace.

Compassion

Compassion is often conflated with empathy, but they are very different impulses. Empathy is the ability to feel and understand the state of mind of another. Compassion is feeling compelled to act on that recognition and to assist.

But empathy is not enough. It is only a step, albeit an important one, on the path to compassion. Paul Bloom's masterful and compelling book, Against Empathy, offers scientific research that supports this claim.

Empathy requires effort; compassion demands action. Indeed, compassion is empathy *in* action. But there are still several important distinctions.

Empathy is subjective; compassion is objective. Empathy is exhausting; compassion is energizing. Empathy is most often singular; compassion is more often plural.

Empathy is the gateway; compassion is *the* way.

For your endeavor to be done with intention and integrity, compassion is required.

And like grace, you must extend compassion to yourself if you are to effectively and honestly extend it to others.

Be compassionate.

Chapter 2 - Values, Talents, & Tribes

As indicated by the Venn diagram in the Introduction, your next endeavor lies at the intersection of who you are, what you're good at, and where you belong.

There are undoubtedly other processes for finding your way to your what's next. But this is the one right in front of you now. And if you employ it, I promise it will change you and move you into the change you seek to make.

The workbook referenced in the Table of Contents is a resource worth working through alongside these chapters.

The journey into "what's next," by definition, never ends. But that's only true if you start in the first place.

Go.

Values

Beliefs are bogus. Values more clearly reveal who you are. Values are a better tool than beliefs for informing your decisions and actions.

Beliefs are assumptions based on limited observations and experience. What's more, these convictions filter through a consciousness prone to confirmation bias. Your opinions feed your need to be "right."

Too often beliefs don't stand up to science or scrutiny. Look at the current state of politics, economics, or social issues, and you'll find *plenty* of certainty and confidence about things that are unproven or untrue.

Values speak to your basic needs as a human being who relies on others. They are born of your experience as a social being. What's more, values are not fixed. They change as your needs and desires change.

Beliefs are fixed, personal, and selfish. Values are fluid, universal, and generous.

Values speak to *who* you are.

Beliefs are, at best, a poor compass for navigating an endeavor. Your values, the guiding principles that you live by, are a much better choice for setting your course and correcting it as you go.

"Character is fate." – Heraclitus

Talents

Skills are overrated. Talents are more useful for building an endeavor worthy of your time and attention.

Skills are things you learned in school or on the job. They're tasks that can be written down, taught, and measured. If a skill can be executed more effectively, efficiently, or cheaply by someone other than you, then it *should* be.

Talents are innate abilities you begin to cultivate the moment you enter the world. They are honed through connection and collaboration. Talents can be common to individuals, but how they are combined and practiced are idiosyncratic.

Skills are acquired, common, and disposable. Talents are accessed, unique, and valuable.

Talents speak to *what* you do.

Skills can be useful to an endeavor but hardly set you apart from the teeming throngs who possess the very same competencies. Talents are assets to seek out and cultivate through work worthy of your abilities.

Tribe

The human urge to gather with others who look, think, and act like us is primal. Belonging is wrapped into the same evolutionary imperative that drives our inherent social instinct.

Seth Godin wrote a book about how to leverage this instinct. Tribes is a short read that pays enormous dividends to those who invest the time to read it, but I'll share a few essential takeaways to serve your purposes here.

Tribes are groups of people connected by an idea and to one another. Members who earn the privilege may temporarily lead them. Tribes share a vision, speak a common language, and can spot the shibboleths and signifiers that distinguish them from outsiders.

A tribe is not an audience. Audiences lack the loyalty required of a tribe. A tribe is not a collection of fans. A tribe is made up of dyed in the wool true believers and evangelicals. A tribe is not a club. Sure, members know the unwritten rules and secret handshakes, but that's because they help create and perpetuate them. Tribal leaders are not famous gurus; they're generous guides.

In identifying your tribe, agreement around core values facilitates cooperation and understanding. These shared values establish your "scene." A place for you to develop and deliver your endeavor. Your tribe will also be made up of collaborators and clients who need your talents to enhance their lives. Your talents are "the gift" you share with the tribe.

Members of your tribe are fellow travelers. The tribe exists to further *every* member's journey and well-being. Generosity and compassion are expected. Promiscuity and posing are frowned upon. Selfishness or manipulation lead to ostracism.

Tribes speak to *where* you belong.

Tribes are *not* to be trifled with. Your ability to thrive depends on the tribe.

Chapter 3 - Orientation & Course Setting

The alignment of who you are, what you're good at, and where you belong positions you to identify the work that you're meant to do now. Clarity in your values, talents, and tribe encourage you to lean into an endeavor with greater intention and integrity.

Now it's time to orient yourself and set a course for your endeavor. Goals, strategy, and tactics are tools that help you do this.

Goals, strategy, and tactics help you step into the difference you seek to make. But these terms are often conflated or confused. Let's define each and explore how to employ them to expedite your endeavor.

Goals

A goal clearly identifies and expresses the transformation you seek to make. Who's it for? What's it for? What does success look and feel like?

Goals are a promise to yourself and others that you can deliver.

Your goal should be stated with clear intention and align with your values, talents, and tribe.

Goals should not be changed often nor ill-advisedly.

Your goal informs and organizes your strategy.

Strategy

A strategy is the primary lever for making progress toward your goal. An effective approach applies tension and status roles as ratchets to help bring about change worth the effort.

Efficient strategies leverage emotional labor, empathy, generosity, trust, permission, enrollment, and investment to make change happen.

A strategy serves your goal and informs and organizes your tactics.

Your strategy must also align with your values, talents, and tribe.

Your strategy should be thought through carefully and should not be changed on a whim or for the sake of expediency. That is the purview of tactics.

Tactics

Tactics are the tools, events, interactions, efforts, and offers that serve your strategy and goal. Tactics are organized by strategy to realize goals.

Tactics are tried, tested, and iterated. The best tactics are elegantly simple. Tactics should be easily executable and measurable. You need to know whether or not a tactic is working.

Ineffective tactics are revised and retested or abandoned. Just because tactics are disposable, doesn't mean they shouldn't be ethically employed or empathetically constructed.

Tactics must also align with your values, talents, and tribe.

Effective tactics are amplified and leveraged until they stop working.

Developing and employing tactics keeps you sharp. Always be testing and analyzing tactics.

Even with the terms clearly defined, it can be challenging to develop and deploy goals, strategy, and tactics. Here are a few case studies to help you see what these terms look like in action.

A hairdresser's goal is to improve the quality of his clientele. His strategy is to create a more premium customer experience. The tactics he tests are upgrading his product line, serving espresso, playing classical music, and increasing pricing.

The goal of parents is to improve connection and communication with their children. The strategy they use is to increase the amount of family time. Their tactics are to schedule nights for screen-free family dinners, a family game night, and a family day trip on weekends.

A local bank executive's goal is to increase her branch's customer base. Her strategy is to become the most trusted bank in town. The tactics she tests are to sponsor teams in the recreational league, invite the chamber of commerce to hold meetings in the branch's boardroom and host a chili cook-off between the fire department and sheriff's office.

My goal with this book is to help you cultivate well-being through meaningful work. My strategy is to earn your trust and encourage you to share the lessons learned here. The tactics I employ are live events, sharing chapters, broadcasting promotional offers, and delivering bonuses to purchasers.

But Will Your Endeavor Take Off?

Ultimately, it is impossible to know if an endeavor will succeed. What does "success" even look like? Too often success is confused with popularity and profits.

What if you measured success by the well-being it generates for yourself and others? What if success is doing well enough today so that you can get up and do it again tomorrow?

Take care of the important things, like maintaining your integrity and stepping forward with intention. The less important things, like how much recognition and reward you receive, will take care of themselves.

One thing is assured. If you never start your endeavor, you'll never know if it has legs. Traction requires movement. If you don't build it, they certainly won't come.

And what if your endeavor fails? Everything you do rubs up against the possibility that it might not work. It's very likely that your effort won't unfold as planned. But that's precisely how integrity and intention are tested and made more resilient.

There are lessons to be learned from *any* outcome. There's also the opportunity to practice the virtues of patience, humility, and acceptance. Any result can be leveraged to build character, courage, and will.

Until you start, you are hiding. Which posture, starting or hiding, comes with the greatest possibility of regret?

The only way to make progress with your endeavor is to lean in and do the work.

"But I haven't figured out what my endeavor is."

I understand. I've been sorting out my current endeavor for years, and it's *still* not completely clear. But one thing is sure; it's clearer today than it was yesterday. I suspect it will be clearer still tomorrow.

When I started my current venture, it wasn't even called *Creative On Purpose*. It didn't look *anything* like it does now.

How did it become a thriving enterprise? It began as a blog. A blog on a platform I didn't even own. This endeavor started with a simple promise to myself that I was going to figure out what this damn thing was about. And I did it by posting a 2-minute read once or twice every week for years.

I paid attention to what resonated with readers and what didn't. I wrote more of what worked and less of what didn't. Short, easily completed habits led to more significant projects. Like a weekly broadcast where I chatted with friends about topics of mutual interest. This led to one-hour workshop webinars, a weekly newsletter, and speaking gigs.

My endeavor wasn't all planned in advance, and when there was a plan, I rarely stuck to it. Sometimes I sailed with the wind, other times I tacked back and forth into it. When I wasn't clear on my intentions, I doubled down on maintaining my integrity.

Day by day, drip by drip, connection by connection, my endeavor became more focused.

And so did I. So can you.

Clarity, relevance, and engagement come when you start where you are and take the next step with integrity and intention.

The time is now. Now is the time.

"But I haven't figured out what my endeavor is." (Take 2)

"Test drive" an endeavor by simply creating a "pretend" one, a practice scenario. Nothing to which you're too attached. You don't even need to base it on anything real. Just make up a project and run it through the process as an exercise.

Developing and delivering an endeavor is like building a muscle. It gets stronger through being exercised.

Less Is More

"To attain knowledge, add things every day. To attain wisdom, remove things every day." - Lao Tzu

This is the hardest lesson I've *ever* learned. In fact, I relearn it *daily*. I'm sharing it with you and *imploring* you to pay attention.

Less is more.

You are born into a world where more isn't enough. This impulse is fueling the woes and suffering you wrestle with today.

As you unpack your endeavor and identify who it's for and what it's for, think small. Keep it simple.

You aren't going to transform the world overnight. Your idea won't become an immediate change agent. Your actions won't instantly initiate a movement.

The cosmos doesn't owe you a thing. But it does reward thoughtful, ethical, and determined effort.

Be deliberate. You can lean in and leap when what's working and what isn't is more clear. Until then, baby steps.

Do only what is necessary and required. Efficiency is elegant.

Less is more.

Your endeavor is not an endeavor until you have your first fans and followers who are not just enrolled in the journey you're leading but are *invested*.

Everyone must be on the hook. There must be shared interests. Stakes are required.

The stakes shouldn't be life or death. But they must speak to and satisfy basic needs and wants. Begin with a small offering that helps fellow travelers take an initial step toward a dream or desire. You can follow up with another. And then another.

Less is more.

Progress is made through precise, persistent, and purposeful pushes.

Book II - Agendas & Attachments

There is *also* an antihero in this endeavor. That would also be you! More specifically, it's the agendas and attachments that hold you back, keep you humble and hiding, and cause you to get in your own way.

Let's investigate these challenges *and* the opportunities within them!

Chapter 4 - Adversaries & Antidotes

Work that makes a difference, by definition, makes change happen. You are engaging in an endeavor to enhance your life by elevating the lives of others. That's a *lot* of transformation to strive for.

And one thing is sure. Certainty and confidence aren't going to help you get there.

That's because certainty and confidence are tools of the status quo. Certainty and confidence imply that you understand a domain or situation. You have every reason to believe you can predict what will happen next. Furthermore, you have a vested interest in having things remain as they are when you are certain and confident.

The thing about work that makes a difference is that you can never be sure it will turn out as planned. In fact, you must embrace the idea that it might not work.

It's time to shun the sure thing and the status quo. Time to boldly leap into the void with an idea that might not work (but then again, just might). Lean into your endeavor, even though it's very likely to not turn out exactly as you imagine.

Against Certainty & Confidence

Traditional social, religious, political, educational, and economic institutions encourage and reward certainty and confidence. These establishments thrive when things are done the same way they've always been done. And those who succeed within these systems do so because they've mastered what's already known.

Traditional organizations and those who thrive in them have a vested interest in certainty and confidence because it serves them. It's a cycle of selfishness that favors those at the top over those who are not.

Innovation in established institutions is hard to come by, and when it does, it happens at a glacial pace. That's because innovation requires trying things that might change the current situation. Are in fact likely to do so.

Testing and trying new ideas requires curiosity, courage, and creativity. Those who have an attachment to the tried and true, and the way things are, are threatened by these impulses and the change they initiate.

Which is the very reason why you *must* cultivate curiosity, courage, and creativity.

Curiosity

Curiosity isn't the opposite of certainty. It exists on a continuum between doubt and certitude.

Curiosity cultivates wonder, inquiry, and delight. It causes an itch. Curiosity feeds a thirst for knowledge. It creates the desire to try, test, and tweak. Curiosity is contagious and causes change.

Be curious.

Courage

Courage is found at the midpoint on the continuum between recklessness and cowardice.

Courage cultivates resolve and resilience. It shuns regret. Courage causes you to scratch the itch initiated by curiosity. It helps turn knowledge into wisdom. Courage impels you to try, test, and tweak. Courage is contagious, and it encourages collaboration.

Be courageous.

Creativity

Creativity lies between conformity and pretension.

This is important. Creativity doesn't happen *to* you. It happens *through* you.

Creativity is fueled by curiosity and powered by imagination. Creativity is "challenge accepted," coupled with the courage to explore, experiment, and educate your way toward a solution.

Creativity is generous and vulnerable. It requires courage. At some point, you and your creation must stand up and be seen or speak up and be heard.

Be creative.

The Perils of Assumptions, Agendas, & Attachments

Assumptions, agendas, and attachments are impediments to your well-being and your ability to enhance the lives of others through your endeavor.

Assumptions are beliefs held to be true without question or proof. They are formed from incomplete, perhaps even incorrect, information. Assumptions are prone to confirmation bias, circular logic, and lazy thinking. Worst of all, assumptions keep you attached to ideas about the past that serves "what is."

Agendas are "to do" lists. They're busy work, tasks not often working toward a meaningful or helpful purpose. Too often an agenda's goal is hidden and selfish. Worst of all, agendas keep you attached to preconceived results in the future that serve the status quo.

Endeavors shun the banal and workaday. The purpose of your enterprise is to learn from the past, enhance the current state of affairs, and strive for a future where more can flourish. Assumptions' attachment to the past and agendas' attachment to the future promote suffering, not satisfaction.

Assumptions, agendas, and attachment are just some of the insidious stories you are told. Even more unacceptable, they're stories you often tell yourself.

Time to commit to telling stories that promote your actual interests and the aspirations of those you serve.

Attachment Vs. Commitment

Is your endeavor something you're attached to or something you're committed to?

Distinguish between commitment and attachment might be helpful.

Commitment is a pledge. An oath to strive for excellence in an endeavor worthy of your time and talent.

Commitment is a promise you are working on *now*.

Attachment is fixating on expectation. Affixing yourself to an idea or outcome.

Attachments are tied to the past or the future.

Two time-tested traditions have much to say on attachment and commitment. The Buddhists say the root of all suffering is attachment. The Stoics say that a commitment to excellence of character is all that is required for happiness.

What attachments can you let go of to thrive more and stress less?

What commitments can you make that will help you to fly higher in an endeavor that matters?

Chapter 5 - The Stories You Tell

Stories are how human beings have *always* connected, communicated, and collaborated. Whether you're promoting, persuading, or pretending, you're simply telling a story.

Storytelling begins with the stories you tell yourself. Those stories inform and influence the stories you tell others.

Stories matter. Stories matter *a lot*. The most important stories are subtle, nuanced, and layered. They're also often fraught with hidden meanings and frequently misconstrued.

Don't just listen *to* the story. Listen *for* the story.

Tell me a story.

What Stories Are You Telling Yourself?

"I'm not good enough." ➡ "I'm a work in progress."

"I'm stuck." ➡ "I'm ready!"

"I can't catch a break." ➡ "There's opportunity in every obstacle."

"I'm scared." ➡ "Isn't that interesting...?"

"No one ever helps me." ➡ "Let's go!"

"I don't deserve more." ➡ "I am worthy."

"I must put my family first." ➡ "I must take care of myself to best serve others."

"I need to learn more." ➡ "I know enough to start."

"I don't know how to start." ➡ "I'll start where I am."

"What if I fail?" ➡ "Failure is not fatal."

"What'll people think?" ➡ "Shun the non-believers."

"I can't afford the time or money." ➡ "I can re-prioritize."

"This is as good as it gets." ➠ "There's always room for improvement."

"What's the point?" ➠ "What's next?"

The stories you tell yourself dictate your worldview and mindset. They inform your attitude and posture. The stories you tell yourself influence how you hear the stories you're told *and* the stories you tell others. The stories you tell yourself determine whether you lean in and leap into your endeavor or cower and hide from it.

Choose your story. Choose your future.

Choose well.

Frame or Reframe?

The stories you tell and listen to, are inspired by your observation and experience. They're informed by your worldview. Stories are framed for effect. Frames are interpretations that influence your perspective and opinion.

That doesn't mean you have to accept either the story or the frame "as is."

If the story you're listening to at any moment isn't serving you. Stop listening to it or reframe it.

Remember, how you choose to see yourself, your surroundings, and your situation is something you have agency over. You don't have to accept a story as gospel or dogma.

Ignore unhealthy and unhelpful stories. Those you can't overlook, reframe into opportunities or lessons.

Fear

Pursuing an endeavor means trying ideas and engaging in activities that are new and might not work. Anytime you're leaning into a new enterprise, especially one you are enrolled and invested in, fear shows up.

Fear keeps you humble and hiding. It intends to keep you anonymous and "safe." Fear doesn't mean to cause you harm.

But denying your desire to develop your excellence and deliver on your promise *does* cause you pain. Self-doubt, self-dramatization, self-medication, self-criticism, and self-imposed isolation and procrastination are common expressions of your struggles with fear.

What to do?

In *The War of Art*, Steven Pressfield gives fear the name Resistance. Seth Godin asserts that fear emanates from your Lizard Brain. Whatever you want to call it, you need to identify fear and then reframe your relationship with it.

Fear is merely a manifestation of anxiety. Anxiety is an expression of suffering that comes from attachment. Attachment to an idea about your value or abilities based on your past or attachment to expectations you have about your future.

Either way, attachment is taking you out of the present moment which is where you have the power to make a choice that better serves your higher interests and well-being. Right now you can choose to be aware of what's going on and reframe your fear into a more healthy, helpful, and true conceptualization.

Instead of confronting fear, why not recognize it for what it actually is? A gentle (or not so gentle), tap on the shoulder letting you know that you're considering an endeavor worth exploring. Fear is a compass pointing out just the right direction for you to lean into next.

You can then acknowledge fear and say, "Thank you. Thank you for revealing that this endeavor is worth considering. That this enterprise is worthy of my time, talent, and effort. Worth stepping into."

And then do that.

Feedback

For your endeavor to thrive, you need to be open to feedback. Indeed, you *must* seek it out. That does *not* mean you must accept every criticism that gets hurled in your direction from every critic who crosses your path.

Criticism and feedback are two very different things.

Criticism, more often than not, is unsolicited and comes from questionable sources with equally questionable agendas. Criticism serves the critic, not you or your work.

Feedback is solicited from trusted and respected sources. Feedback is delivered with love and intended to help improve and elevate your endeavor.

Criticism comes from naysayers and non-believers. Feedback comes from real fans of and true believers in your endeavor.

Shun the non-believers. Seek the true believers.

Failure

Endeavors by definition are new or innovative. This means that they might not work. New ideas and activities are indeed unlikely to work right away. And yet, when done with integrity and intention, they may well work out.

Failure in developing and delivering your endeavor is inevitable. There will be mistakes, misconceptions, and missteps. Reframed, these "failures" are invaluable insights, lessons, and opportunities.

The information failure shares provide food for thought about how your endeavor can be iterated and improved. A failure supplies knowledge that informs pivots, better directions, and perhaps more fitting approaches.

Failure also has real benefits. Failure cultivates resilience, sharpens the focus, and fuels resolve.

Failure isn't fatal. Failure is your friend. It's not an enemy to fight or run away from, failure is an ally to embrace and understand.

"Ever tried. Ever failed. No matter. Try again. Fail again. Fail better." - Samuel Beckett

Forward

Forward is the posture of those who endeavor.

Yet, fear, feedback, and failure often paralyze. These impulses pull you away from your experience in stepping forward and into your head and then into your own way. Fear, feedback, and failure can dull your enthusiasm and fuel inertia.

You must maintain forward motion if your endeavor is to progress.

Reframing fear, feedback, and failure turn them into valuable assets for developing and delivering endeavors that make a difference. Reframing is simple. But simple is rarely easy.

That's why you need fellow travelers.

Fellow Travelers

Remember that your endeavor is done *with* and *for* others. Seek them out sooner rather than later. Your tribe is already gathered. If you haven't found them yet, now is the time.

Surrounding yourself with friends diminishes the power of fear. Your tribe is a source for useful feedback. Failure doesn't hurt nearly as much when you're surrounded by family.

Find the others. Gather the clan. Fellow travelers fuel forward motion.

What Are You Waiting For?

Getting your ducks in a row?

Your ship to come in?

The planets to align?

The "right" time?

The ducks will line themselves up. You don't even own a ship. And, when was the last time you took the time to check on the planets?

Time is everyone's most valuable resource. You're never going to have more of it than you do right now. Why are you wasting it?

Every moment of every day is another step toward your ultimate end.

The time is now. Now is the time.

> *"While we wait for life, life passes." - Seneca*

Chapter 6 - Perception & Perspective

Perception is understanding. Perspective is outlook. Both are important.

"Know thyself" is an ancient aphorism about self-perception worth contemplating. "The golden rule" is an ancient maxim common to many religions and traditions worth practicing that provides a perspective about how to treat others.

It's challenging to get clear about the motivation, aim, and aspiration for an endeavor.

Here are some questions worth considering before you begin:

What's your motivation? What's the point? Are you sure about the transformation you seek to facilitate? Do you have a definite audience in mind?

What's your aim? Is the benefit you're promising explicit? Does your goal align with your values and talents?

What's your aspiration? What does "success" look and feel like for those you seek to serve? What does "success" look and feel like to you?

The ancient philosopher, Socrates, took the "know thyself" statement even further by declaring, "The unexamined life is not worth living."

Whether you agree with that assertion or not, it might be worth asking yourself, "Is the unexamined endeavor worth doing?"

Perspective and perception matter.

Prestige & Prosperity

Fame and fortune are seductive, and deceptive, pursuits. They might be side-effects of an endeavor worth your time and talents, but they aren't necessary or even likely results of work worth doing.

What's more, fame is no measure of value or worth and fortune is no measure of achievement or success.

Instead, consider prestige and prosperity.

Prestige is the distinction earned through your efforts of being recognized and sought out by the *right* people. The people who care. The people who need what you offer.

Prosperity is earning enough through your efforts to be able to get up the next morning and do it again.

Passion & Purpose

Passion is misunderstood.

Passion is often seen as something that you must bring *to* an endeavor. Which means that first, you have to find it.

Passion is actually something that is cultivated *through* meaningful work.

When you approach your endeavor for a purpose, with purpose, and on purpose, passion results. So does an even greater sense of purpose.

Endeavors are inherently fraught with difficulties and challenges. And these efforts take time. Usually, more time than you initially think.

If you're lucky enough to know your passion, great. But if you rely on it to power you through the process of developing and delivering your endeavor, you're mining passion like a finite resource.

The thing about a finite resource is that it can run out before you complete your work. Better to fuel your enterprise with a renewable energy source.

Purpose is not only a renewable resource but a resilient one. Fuel your endeavor with purpose and passion is a likely by-product. Which turns passion also into a renewable resource that can continue to fuel your project as it unfolds and thrives.

Pursuit & the Point

As your endeavor journey unfolds, at some point (more likely at many points), you'll find yourself asking this question (or a variation on it), "What's the point?"

Spending time with the questions posed at the beginning of this book may help you continue to find meaning and pursue your endeavor with purpose. You might also consider that the pursuit itself may be the point.

In many traditions, the point of worthy pursuits is not human *doing* but rather human *being*. The quest to become more human. The search for wisdom.

"Knowledge speaks. Wisdom listens."

Knowledge is a process of acquiring and adding. Wisdom is a process of distillation and understanding.

Knowledge or wisdom? Choose your pursuit, choose your point.

Build Yourself from the Ground Up

Your life, your work, your year. When you look back at each of these, you can lose sight that they are built from months, days, hours, and minutes.

But it's in each moment that you have an opportunity to start, or try, or test.
Each juncture provides an opportunity to face obstacles, misfortunes, and challenges with greater clarity and equanimity.

Each instant is a chance for you to succeed or fail, but also to learn, to grow. The opportunity for you to develop yourself.

And the next moment is your next chance to start again, or restart, or quit, or pivot, or change course.

And that's how every endeavor is built. How each project, your life's work, and your very life itself is constructed. Goal by goal. Action by action. Result by result.

Accepting what comes and then deciding what to do next.

Living and working moment to moment interrupts the voice of doubt living in your head. The self-critic, the over-planner, and the over-thinker that tries to hijack your efforts to do work worth doing.

You decide how to interpret your current situation or circumstance. You choose what to do next. You decide what to build, how to make it, when to start it, and with whom and for whom to construct it.

So, lace up your work boots and grab your work gloves. It's time to get to work. Start building right now.

"You must build up your life action by action, and be content if each one achieves its goal as far as possible - and no one can keep you from this. But there will be some external obstacle! Perhaps, but no obstacle to acting with justice, self-control, and wisdom. But what if some other area of my action is thwarted? Well, gladly accept the obstacle for what it is and shift your attention to what is given, and another action will immediately take its place, one that better fits the life you are building." - Marcus Aurelius, Meditations

The Virtues (& Vices) of Thrashing

In any endeavor worthy of your time and talents you'll face challenges, obstacles, and problems. There's a time and there's a place for educating yourself, preparing, and planning for these moments. There's *also* a time to dive in and thrash your way to clarity and resolution.

Thrashing is the process of learning, iterating, and improving by doing. This needs to be done strategically, with intention, and in service to the change, you seek to make. Without having a goal in mind and a clear idea of what success looks and feels like, thrashing can become exhausting and frustrating.

Thrashing can also become a seductive invitation to hide in busy-work and avoid the more important emotional labor of connecting and collaborating with those who need you.

Done well and done right, thrashing can be exhilarating and encourage a greater sense of flourishing. In addition to bringing your endeavor into clearer focus, this approach encourages forward motion and builds resilience.

If the term "thrashing" doesn't resonate, replace it with "dancing," "testing," or any other word that works for you.

Whatever you want to call it, here are some further tips for effective and efficient thrashing.

- Know what your thrashing is for. Have a specific goal in mind and a clear idea of what success looks and feels like.
- Know who your thrashing is for. It's for those you seek to serve. The sooner you gain clarity on who that is and how you can enhance their lives the sooner you can all thrive more and stress less.
- Know what the promise of thrashing is. If done early, quickly, and intentionally, thrashing will help you make the most of what you have and where you're at now.

Again, thrash early and only as often as necessary, but most of all thrash with intention and integrity.

All Is Lost

At some point, if your pursuit is serious and significant, you will find yourself confronting a moment of doubt, perhaps even despair. Your endeavor will face a necessary and essential trial. A moment when it appears that all is lost.

It's tempting to call this moment a "gut check." I'd rather call it a "moment of truth." Sometimes it makes sense to quit. Sometimes the only choice is to continue.

The all is lost moment will test your resolve and your reserves. This moment also requires that you decide if it's time to quit or continue.

It's okay to pause and ask yourself, and others, some critical questions. Does your endeavor still align with your values, talents, and tribe? Does it still delight you, or does it leave you depleted? Does it energize or enervate you? Is it contributing to your well-being and that of others?

It's also necessary to set a deadline. A date in the very near future where you *must* decide to continue or quit. An all is lost moment always precedes the climax of a story or an endeavor.

This is not a do or die moment. It's merely the moment when you must choose what's next.

And there's *always* a what's next.

Book III - Acceptance & Ascent

Where you, the hero of your endeavor, are forever transformed, and share your endeavor and the lessons learned with your tribe. Your life and that of those you care about are enhanced through your pursuit.

Chapter 7 - Assertions & Acknowledgement

The antidote to assumptions and agendas are assertions

The solution to suffering and struggle is acknowledgment.

Assertions

Assertions are ideas held to be true based on your observation and experience. When you put them forth to be "tested," you open the door to engage and understand someone else's point of view and experience. You're also afforded the opportunity to improve your good ideas and abandon your bad ones.

Assertions employ your curiosity and courage. They help you avoid the pitfalls of certainty and over-confidence. Assertions help you stop talking at, to, over, past, around, and through others and instead engage in collaborative conversation with them.

Assertions also help foster acknowledgment. Acknowledgment of others and other ideas. When your statements collide with the claims of others, they may not stand up to scrutiny. Your assertions may be revealed to be weak or even wrong.

You then have the opportunity to acknowledge a better conception of what is true. You can abandon outdated ideas and begin building new assertions that are better and stronger.

Through assertions, you can begin to acknowledge being right or wrong with equal humility, gratitude, and equanimity.

Acknowledgment

Assertions aren't a sign of weakness or lack of will. Acceptance of what happens doesn't make you a doormat. Assertions are an expression of having the curiosity to investigate ideas. They also require the courage to acknowledge fact and fiction.

Acknowledging the true, the false, or the ambiguity of an assertion implies that you're ready to stop railing against what *is* and start stepping into what *can be*.

Embracing assertions and acknowledging what they reveal promotes well-being and inspires forward motion and flying higher. Recognizing the power of assertions and the necessity of acceptance is the path to progress and ascent.

Fate or Free Will?

Is "what happens next" due to fate or the exercise of your free will?

It's comforting to believe you control what happens next. But do you? What if what happens next has already been decided? What if *everything* that happens is fated?

"My formula for greatness in a human being is amor fati: that one wants nothing to be different, not forward, not backward, not in all eternity." - Friedrich Nietzsche

Why not love fate? A life that is fated does *not* imply that it just happens *to* you. Life also happens *through* you.

In a fated cosmos, you may be a tiny cog in the machinery of the universe, but you still have a vital role to play.

Past events alone don't determine your future. You can, and should, be an active participant in your life *now*. How your life proceeds may be fated, but it also reflects your character. Why not do your best and let what unfolds be what it will be?

Acceptance of what happens next is the path to well-being in your endeavor. This doesn't make you a doormat. It's a measure of your character. Accepting what is allows you to decide what's next with deliberation and determination.

Hardship is inevitable. Suffering is a choice. Attachment to past outcomes and future expectations are the path to suffering. Suffering is self-imposed punishment and imprisonment.

The past is fixed. The future is uncertain. Only in the here and now, the present moment, do you possess agency.

If you cannot absolutely know or control what happens next, why not act "as if?" Step into what's next with intention and integrity "fate permitting."

The result of your effort is not the reward; the reward is the opportunity in front of you.

Fate or free will? The answer matters less than the quality of your choice and virtue of your effort.

Chapter 8 - Accountability & Aptitude

"Learning that does not lead to action is useless." - Epictetus

In the pursuit of your endeavor, you will have to stand up and be seen and speak up and be heard. You will be making promises to others and yourself. You will be putting yourself "on the hook."

You must embrace accountability if you're going to make a difference.

Own your successes, but don't exult too long. Each achievement is merely another step toward the higher goal of making a more significant impact.

Take responsibility for your failures, but never despair. Failures are lessons to be embraced that cultivate resolve and resilience.

Accountability is the path to aptitude. Competence leads to proficiency which leads to mastery and ultimately excellence.

Posture

Posture is "adopting the approach of a _____."

You can fill in the blank with any of many roles or positions.

Committing to a posture is like trying on an outfit and walking around in it for a while. It's a test drive, not a life sentence. Committing to a posture with intention may shorten the "shopping trip" to find a long-term posture.

What posture does your endeavor require? The posture of a leader? Teacher? Bootstrapper? Partner? Explorer? Parent?

Any of these postures, or any other required of a worthy endeavor, require embracing your curiosity and engaging your courage.

Composer or Arranger?

The composer knows the rules. He's studied and done his homework. He writes well-crafted arrangements. Specific and carefully chosen instructions are included. The work of a composer reflects his character and purpose, especially when played by those who know how to do as instructed.

The improviser has the same training, but a different approach. She understands the structure and intent of a piece *and* sees the possibilities. The improviser's stance is, "Let's play with this and see what we can come up with." She serves the song but isn't enslaved by it.

Composition and improvisation are equally professional approaches to the same situation. There's a time and there's a place for composing, especially when you want things to turn out as expected. But when you want to investigate and innovate, the improviser's process is better suited for that endeavor.

The composer relies on what's been done. The improvise leans into "what's next."

Composer or improviser. Which posture should you adopt now?

Of Shame & Sufficiency

Shame is an invitation you do *not* have to accept.

There is *no* shame in sufficiency.

You are sufficient even as you strive.

Of Shame

You can't advance an endeavor without making mistakes. Getting things "right" involves going through a lot of "wrong."

And some of those "wrong" choices come with a heaping helping of regret. And when regret appears, you can be sure that shame is following close behind.

But here's the thing, when shame comes to visit, you don't have to extend it an invitation to stay for a week or even overnight. You're not required to ask shame to lunch or tea.

Don't draw the shades and lock the door. That only encourages shame to hang around. And shame is very patient and extremely persistent.

Instead, meet shame at the door and thank it.

"Thank you, Shame, for coming by. Your presence indicates I have work to do. A mistake to own, an apology and amends to make. Sitting with you, for even a minute, will only get in the way of the important work I must do. So, thanks again for stopping by, I'm quite sure I'll be seeing you again."

Then practice the 4 Rs of an intentional, healing, and meaningful apology: recognize that you're wrong, take responsibility, express your regret, do what you can to make it right. Then move on to what's next.

Mistakes are inevitable. Shame is a choice.

Of Sufficiency

Building your endeavor is a rigorous pursuit. Most anything worth doing is.

And it's "voluntary." You enrolled and invested in this journey, but you're certainly under no obligation to keep it up or keep at it.

But for those who want to do either, it's easy to get bogged down.

You observe. You create. You share. You receive insights, questions, alternative perspectives, pushback, and encouragement. You rethink, review, revise, reshare.

You get more feedback. Do more rethinking. Maybe some doubt creeps into your thinking. Maybe some inertia seeps into your posture. It can get overwhelming.

What to do?

Keep flying higher.

You don't need to "get it right." Not right now. Just get it "alright" for right now.

There are no ultimate right answers or interpretations. An endeavor is as much a work in progress as you are.

Deeper understanding and greater clarity of the concepts come as you proceed. Experiences build each on the next. The lessons learned fit together like puzzle pieces.

You can always circle back. Perhaps you'll do so with a fresh perspective, an understanding of "the bigger picture." Maybe even a new approach.

You're in flight. It may feel like your thrashing. Even falling. But you're actually flying.

And you become a stronger flyer by continuing to fly.

Keep flying higher.

Chapter 9 - Sweeping the Floor

You live in a time and place that appears to reward those who get things done. So you are encouraged to be productive and to follow checklists, complete "to do" lists, and to employ productivity tricks and hacks.

But tricks aren't real and who wants to be a hack?

Endeavors are enterprises that are worth it. The sort of efforts worth your attention *and* worthy of your time and talents. It's work that transforms you as you enhance the lives of others.

This kind of undertaking never really ends. It's not "one and done." In any given moment you will find yourself in different circumstances and situations, surrounded by new people, and in novel and distinct places.

You are a different person today than you were yesterday. You will be a different person again tomorrow.

You never step into the same river twice. You and your endeavor are works in progress.

You don't sweep a floor once and never return to sweep it again. You revisit the process repeatedly. You come back again and again mindfully, presently, and with intention and gratitude.
Like any endeavor, sweeping the floor is its own reward.

Resilience & Resolve

Challenge and hardship are inevitable. Struggle and suffering are choices.

So are resilience and resolve.

Progress is facilitated when training is put into practice. You *need* obstacles, challenges, and misfortune that test and push your abilities.

Don't avoid these moments. Don't hide from them. Welcome them. Embrace them. Thank them.

People, situations, and circumstances that encourage you to exercise and employ what you've learned are why you practice and prepare. You'll grow, or you'll learn.

Either is a lesson in resilience and resolve that's worth your time and effort.

"What man actually needs is not a tensionless state but rather the striving and struggling for some goal worthy of him."—*Viktor Frankl*

The Games You Play

With your endeavor, are you playing a finite game or an infinite game?

James Carse's short book, *Finite and Infinite Games*, is worth reading.

A finite game has clear rules and ends with clear winners and real losers. Winning a finite game means following the rules. Do as you're told, get schooled, get a job, get promoted, get married, have kids, buy a big house, buy a lot of stuff, etc. This game ends in fortune and status.

That is if you win.

But for you and your "team" to win, others and their team must lose.

You know people who are playing the finite game of life. Are they the happiest, healthiest, and most human folks you know?

A finite game isn't very satisfying because it's out of alignment with our natural impulse to be present, practice gratitude, and serve others.

An infinite game has a different intent, to be able to keep playing. This can only happen if those you are playing with can keep playing, too.

In the infinite game approach to life, the point is for all to thrive and prosper. To do that means everyone playing has a vested interest in helping the other players succeed and flourish as well.

The object isn't "winning" or "getting it right." All you need to do is get it right enough to be able to play again tomorrow. If you're intentional and play with integrity, you'll do so and be both wiser and more skilled.

You enhance your life by improving the lives of others. Aligning your interests with those of others leads to greater fulfillment and happiness. Everyone wins.

You're already a player in the endeavor game. Which game are you playing?

The Archer

Approach your endeavor in the same manner as an archer approaches her craft.

The archer chooses her equipment with deliberation. She maintains the bow and arrows with care. The archer practices daily. She seeks out mentors to learn from.

She also teaches those who are not as skilled and trains with her equals. The archer tends to her physical, mental, and spiritual health.

When the archer aims at her target, she understands what is, and is not, within her control. She controls her preparation and she controls her effort. She's in charge of her thoughts and actions up to the moment the arrow is released.

The archer also knows what is *not* within her control. She does not control the outcome of her efforts. A sudden wind may rise and blow the arrow off target. A rival may cheat. Her equipment or her training may fail.

When the archer notches the arrow, draws back the bowstring, takes aim, and lets the arrow fly, her sole goal is putting forth the best *effort* she is capable of *in that moment*.

The archer has *nothing* invested in the *result* other than the lessons she learns. If she fails to hit the bullseye, she will not despair. If she does pierce it, she will not excessively exult.

The endeavor is its own reward.

Postscript - The Final Flourish

A 100-year-old Stayman Winesap apple tree in full bloom is a pretty majestic sight. That's all my wife and I remembered from a tour of the 38-acre farm in Check, Virginia that we purchased soon afterward.

We raised our two sons there, in addition to dogs, cats, chickens, fruit trees, berry bushes, a vegetable garden and more than a few eyebrows.

Every year the apple tree bore fruit in such abundance that we couldn't keep up with processing and canning apples or pressing them into cider. The boys spent endless hours climbing that tree. My wife spent countless hours gazing out at it from her office window.

One spring, the apple tree was so loaded with blooms that it visibly vibrated with the pollination activity of bees. The limbs became so loaded with apples that they had to be propped up with two-by-fours.

The very next year the tree was obviously in distress. It appeared to be dying. My wife and I, and our boys, were devastated.

We called the county agricultural agent out to take a look and see if there was anything we could do to save our beloved tree. After taking a long look, he explained that the previous year had been the tree's "final flourish." Its last-ditch effort to put out as much fruit as possible. The apple tree's last attempt to realize its purpose.

The tree never put out another apple. A few years later, dead and rotting from within, it toppled over during a severe storm.

This happened as my 50th birthday approached. I was contemplating both my own mortality and my purpose. The tree's demise put a fine point on my thoughts. How was I going to develop and deliver on my potential? What endeavor could I engage in that would tap my promise and nourish others?

You don't know when your last moment will be. However, at this moment recognize that it will come. Begin an endeavor to fulfill your purpose, develops your potential, and taps your promise. It may not yet be time for your final flourish, but it is time to thrive more through work aligned with your values, talents, and tribe. It's time to make a difference through work that matters. It's time to choose your next endeavor.

Ready?

Go.

About the Author of *Endeavor* & Founder of Creative On Purpose

Scott Perry is a husband, father, teacher, and musician from Floyd, Virginia. He coaches in Seth Godin's online programs and is the founder of Creative On Purpose. Scott is also the author of *The Stoic Creative Handbook.*

Endeavor is based on Scott's experience in building a fulfilling and prosperous career as a professional musician, teacher, and consultant. *The Stoic Creative Handbook* shares how an enduring ancient philosophy of life can promote well-being and prosperity while navigating the challenges of an artist's journey.

Made in the USA
Columbia, SC
19 June 2019